ALL OF THE ABOVE

BARNARD NEW WOMEN POETS SERIES
Edited by Christopher Baswell and Celeste Schenck

ALL OF THE ABOVE

DOROTHY BARRESI

With an Introduction by Olga Broumas

BEACON PRESS   BOSTON

Beacon Press
25 Beacon Street
Boston, Massachusetts 02108

Beacon Press books
are published under the auspices of
the Unitarian Universalist Association of Congregations.

98 97 96 95 94 93 92 91   8 7 6 5 4 3 2 1

Text design by Lisa Diercks

Library of Congress Cataloging-in-Publication Data

Barresi, Dorothy.
    All of the above / Dorothy Barresi;
   with an introduction by Olga Broumas.
        p.   cm. — (Barnard new women poets series)
    ISBN 0-8070-6814-4 (cloth). — ISBN 0-8070-6815-2 (pbk.)
    I. Title.   II. Series.
    PS3552.A7326A78   1991
    811'.54—dc20   90-20532
                                          CIP

For My Parents,

Mary Lenore O'Loughlin
Charles Maggio Barresi

CONTENTS

ACKNOWLEDGMENTS

Grateful acknowledgment is made to the editors of the following journals in which these poems first appeared:

AWP Chronicle: "Bombay Hook Wildlife Refuge"
Blue Buildings: "The Judas Clock"
College English: "Vacation, 1969"
Crazyhorse: "Straw Into Gold," "Venice Beach: Brief Song"
Cream City Review: "At the Pioneer Valley Legal Clinic"
Denver Quarterly: "Cinderella and Lazarus, Part II"
The Minnesota Review: "Calvin Coolidge Asleep"
The Pennsylvania Review: "Live Remote"
Ploughshares: "How It Comes," "The Hole in the Ceiling"
Poetry: "Chin Music," "Comeuppance," "Late Summer News,"
   "Lifting," "Nine of Clubs, Cleveland, Ohio"
Poetry Northwest: "Group Therapy Lounge. Columbia, South
   Carolina," "Last Names," "Mystery," "Renoir's *The Luncheon
   of the Boating Party,*" "Thanksgiving"
Shankpainter: "The Registry of Walls and Edges," "Three or Four
   Stars, The Far-Branching Bark of a Dog"
Southern Poetry Review: "In Waking Words"
Tendril: "Large Families"
Willow Springs: "Honeymoon Ocean, 1939"

A number of these poems also appeared in *The Judas Clock,* a limited edition chapbook from the Devil's Millhopper Press, 1986. "Bombay Hook Wildlife Refuge" appears in *New Voices: Selected University & College Prize Winning Poems,* edited by Donald Hall for the Academy of American Poets, 1989. It was awarded a 1983 Anniversary Award by the Associated Writing Programs.

Thanks to Yaddo, the Fine Arts Work Center in Provincetown, the North Carolina Arts Council, and California State University, Northridge, for their generous support and encouragement.

Special thanks to Olga Broumas.

INTRODUCTION
Olga Broumas

The purpose of poetry is to render us speechless, its magic that it should do so by apparent speech. If poetry teaches us anything, Stanley Kunitz has said, it is that we can believe in at least two contradictory things at the same time. I think it begins to teach us that in its first few syllables, by marrying the brain of speech to the brain of music, and through that act unifying the disparates, hope and despair, sufficiency and longing, arrogance and humility, cosmos and self.

Cosmos originally meant ornament, witness *cosmetics;* our ancestors had no fear of the petty leavening the large, though in itself that distinction belies how far we've come, or fallen, since then. Last night, asleep by Dorothy Barresi's manuscript, troubled by the contradiction of having to speak, in prose, about what renders me speechless in her work, I dreamt I was in a little jewelry shop, in a rundown section of Jerusalem, waiting out the slow day with the keepers, mother and daughter. They wanted to know, with the simple curiosity of the deeply faithful, what I believed in. We were speaking in Greek. I said I believed that human beings were imperfect, the word for that being *unfinished,* that we were alive because we were unfinished, and that, since god was life, embracing the imperfect was embracing god. I normally speak English in my dreams so another language inscribes its effort on my consciousness, and I woke with the sequence as vivid as the crumpled pages of Barresi's poems, her sturdy, insolent, bedraggled dancers

> older than God, than dirt,
>
> doing the Lindy, the Bop, the oh

restless for consummation tango.
Not now death; but now, *now.*

I might have said survival, but now I say life buzzes the
bones of these poems, greedy, incessant, voluble, flaunting its
flaws like great hungry mouthfuls torn from the rib of the divine.

>Which is why I don't see but nearly
>collide with the young Mexican woman
>dangling a child by his ankles, headfirst
>
>into the garbage dumpster by my car.
>I'd say *son,* but who can read family for sure
>in a tiny pair of grubby denims, no socks,
>
>and the look she doesn't give me
>which is pure adrenalin, black, *don't say a word.*
>I don't. What is there to say?
>
>. . . . So she fishes
>the little guy deeper, this way and that,
>exhorting him in the Spanish I don't have
>
>until Budweiser cans and redeemable diet
>Cherry 7-Up cans come spinning at her feet,
>and flies rise ecstatic there, big as dimes.

Lest Barresi mythologize, she goes on to place herself, and anyone
with the leisure to be reading this poem, squarely in the compro-
mised position of the semiprivileged, able to observe and only
imperfectly able to redress, yet not giving in to the paralysis of
doing nothing because she can do only a little.

Dorothy Barresi's *little,* her witness, is brash American
primitive, schooled by instant culture and deep immigrant roots,

ricocheting like a pinball between polarities, unwilling to choose
between the sentimental and the sublime, the high-toned and the
sloppy, the historical and the anecdotal. She takes great risks,
attached to her momentum perilously, acrobatically

> . . . listening to the rain as it hangs
> in the pawnshop of those brief trees
> asking for everything . . .

for all that dwells above the zero ground of death,

> . . . housewife to an act that pays and pays and pays.
> Under lights hotter than God
> I activate the angels in my voice and take
> three steps backward, *cha cha cha.*
> But I call it a science more mine
> than either sex or shame
> to be this alone, in time, among others.
> Some days I get up before noon just to hear
> the first notes of the treble world
> break from my throat
> over the heads of everyone listening but me.

Her hunger is contagious and joyous. She celebrates even
what she deplores, embodying in a street-savvy accumulation of
insight Wendell Berry's dictum that "the possible is infinite in the
mind, finite in the world. But to fulfill the possible is to enlarge
it." Of the necrotic ambiance in a Cleveland "Euro" disco, she
observes

> I think this is the end of immigration.

I think if a live pig were thrown
skating and shitting onto the gorgeous dancefloor,
no one would stop posing, or crouch down,

knife between his teeth
and stroking the smooth parquet croon
hunger, hunger, hunger

in his blood's first language. . . .

dignifying by her attention an ennui a lesser person, and I count
myself as such, might have distanced from, dismissed, or ser-
monized by a grimaced lip, an upward roll of the eye.

Dorothy Barresi's sermon—engaged, musical, insistent,
plethoric—is a sassy and spirited embrace of the actual, in its
idiosyncratic improbable splendor. Her humility knows nothing
requires her agreement. Her achievement is to raise from that icy
fact a song ornamented by the polluted trappings that defy it.
Because

Hope is like that. Blind and bleached white,
revising itself every million years
to climb out of the crazy swamp and live.
At the Used Car Lot
day-glo flags are snapping and popping 24 hours,
and you ride that rhythm
in a prone position. They wave
their mutant arms to you,
and you can't help it, down on the mortal sidewalk—
you wave back, astonished as anyone.

ALL OF THE ABOVE

The milkie way, the bird of Paradise,
        Church-bels beyond the starres heard, the souls bloud,
    The land of spices, something understood.
                —George Herbert
                    "Prayer (I)"

Rave on!
            —Buddy Holly

THE BACK-UP SINGER
for C., for the original Coconuts

The Father of the Stethoscope:
René Theophile Hyacinthe Laënnec,
mellifluous name.
In 1816 he rolled a *cornet de papier,* then held it
against the first chest
of the first heart to open its argument
to another man that way, through flesh
and conducting bone. Later
the instrument was crafted of wood, and a small hole bored
for the passage of human sound.

Is it wrong to want to be the only one?
To wish the wedding ring of the spotlight
slipped over me in a moment
that finally holds?
Houselights rise then lower like the rush of blood
through narrowed vessels.
The cymbal solo and high hat
shimmer me forward, but in the blur
and slip of horns I'm singing *do wop*
and *shing, shing-a-ling*
behind a lame pimp and his big-haired girls.

I like to read the old school books.
The page of René Laënnec
turned down in particular, and nearly worn through,
which is also the nature of hope.
A young girl's hands turned
whole lifetimes down.

I'd listen to the telegraphing night bugs'
double ardor, and eventually to darkness
siphoned off by dawn
like the sounds I'd make with my perfect pitch
and years of training under that same blue
no-protection sky.

But there are planetary systems in the blood.
A grand opera of fate brings chances
we can't see but choose somehow.
Later, we see how we went wrong.
Now August says he never, ever
wanted anyone so badly. But there's rehab first,
and the business with his wife.
And the last abortion having left
a disability of my womb
I've come to think of as a million tiny birdsfeet tracking
over muddied ground. Some nights

it's too much like this
on the girls' bus. Regret or Spend It Now,
towels around our throats.
More often it's regret
rolling its bullet casings at our feet—
Lissanne, Yvette, me—
its spent and blackened flashbulbs.
Then I recall the lessons I never quite learned
for their sweetness alone.
On a single mating flight
the queen bee will store enough spermatozoa
to hold her the rest of her working days.

In the blue runways of iris and morning glory,
from ultraviolet
nectar guides, she'll fertilize as she goes.

Call it love that keeps me here.
Call it the final, female talent for demurring
when life takes over.
I call it a living, discovering at sixteen
that come in my mouth doesn't taste
remotely like white flowers.
Ten years later I'm waiting for the bus to stop
or lurch me to my next home.

I'm housewife to an act that pays and pays and pays.
Under lights hotter than God
I activate the angels in my voice and take
three steps backward, *cha cha cha.*
But I call it a science more mine
than either sex or shame
to be this alone, in time, among others.
Some days I get up before noon just to hear
the first notes of the treble world
break from my throat
over the heads of everyone listening but me.

STRAW INTO GOLD

Is the work of this world bitter
but tidy, too? Companionable in its way?
Webs across my doorway

are the dropcloths of persistent
graveyard shifters:
these spiders wish me no harm, gone by 6:32 A.M.

But strands stick in my eyelashes and bangs,
I'm nearly late—stupid, stupid—
and cursing the strong urine by the curb,

the swoonsmell of night-blooming jasmine,
and coffee sloshes over
my lead-bottomed commuter's cup, Have a Special Day.

Which is why I don't see but nearly
collide with the young Mexican woman
dangling a child by his ankles, headfirst

into the garbage dumpster by my car.
I'd say *son,* but who can read family for sure
in a tiny pair of grubby denims, no socks,

and the look she doesn't give me
which is pure adrenalin, black, *don't say a word.*
I don't. What is there to say?

Dim seagulls who routinely mistake
half-defeated neighborhoods like this
for Pacific Ocean

need oiling; they're squealing again.
Without wrath or mercy it seems,
but like all the broken theories and weak

planks of sunlight in my mouth just now,
they build the workdays
we sign our names to, and cross over,

and cross over. So she fishes
the little guy deeper, this way and that,
exhorting him in the Spanish I don't have

until Budweiser cans and redeemable diet
Cherry 7-Up cans come spinning at her feet,
and flies rise ecstatic there, big as dimes.

I'm in my car by now, nothing fancy.
It's a four-door because I've somehow recently passed
into the clear age and zone

of dependable transportation,
and every month a bill
reminding me of the rate of exchange

for a little peace of mind on the freeways.
I remember the kid at the dealership.
Believe it or not, someone

I'd babysat years before, in another lifetime,
with one of those skim-milk mustaches now
and eel-skin cowboy boots.

"Exotics," he called them.
He was proud of those boots. *We've got,* he said,
leaning forward as though to conduct me

on the last forced march of happiness
through the last free world,
a rebate situation

I think you can live with.
And he was right, pretty much. Which is why
even now I'm careful to warm up the engine

before backing out.
I square my briefcase on the seat beside me,
check my lipstick, too,

making two or three big smacking
smooches for the rearview mirror. Pretend ones,
so that anyone seeing me must think

I am two confused people at once.
The tough one blowing goodbye kisses—
so long, suckers!—and the other one,

who touches her white face
to the wheel for a second, that's all,
then sets out for the outskirts of the kingdom
on time, and with proper gifts.

IN WAKING WORDS

for instance, for instance
My mother asleep at the kitchen table
is a commuter except
she is already at home, at work.
Her cheek skims a basket of married socks,
gold toe, green toe, heel and toe,
and I am tapdancing in her big belly, my hands
making S-shapes in the water.
Also brothers orbit there, or the idea of them
encoded, little sputniks.

But who wound the pets up so tight?
It is the fifties, the suburbs. Asleep,
the dog with pink lips and the cat with black lips
twitch on cold linoleum.
The refrigerator is so turquoise it hurts.
And this, too, you'll recognize
if I tell it right.
A child hit by a joyriding Caddy, circa fins,
is suddenly bounceable, laughing,
and because this is a dream,
thrown clear to the female grass.

What my mother wouldn't give
to have that dream again.
What I wouldn't give to have it for her.
But chaos demands space, and things lost
have a life of their own
long after we've stopped searching.

On her stove, a black-and-white flecked tea kettle
is whistling *here lies,*
ready to melt down onto the burner
and become event: metal, gone stars.

LIVE REMOTE
Puritan Road, November 24, 1963

There are thorns, a tiny cyclone fence
surrounding the open heart
of Jesus on the refrigerator.
But to that openness,
to that gilded, blue-tipped, ghost-shaped flame
& teardrops of blood
rolling down his glorious tunic,
perfect as what's painted
on my sister's stupid dolly's face—to all of these
doings in his chest
he points with the mildest agony.
There is nothing shocking
left in the world:
                    here is a Sunday with no cartoons.

No cartoons!
Mother's eyes are rimmed in red; she's pregnant again.
On a sofa locked with eagles
and cracked bells in the Liberty Weave,
her shaky towers rise.
Sheets and towels, mostly. Diapers.
We're orphans to the way
she folds inside herself,
each white flag raised and held a moment longer
than anyone in this outpost
of neediness can bear.
In blue-white tones the screen describes
the circumference of an exit wound
or a pillbox hat.

But Mother is a dreamy girl again
on Chicago's West Side,
feeding cake from her fingertips to the laughing
white-shoed academy boys.

                    Not this ragged crew.
This nightmare of attempted forgetting
and only my brothers in Batman jammies
crying lunch, lunch.
My sister tests the doneness
of Patrick's fingers in her easy bake oven,
first the left hand, then the right.
Me? I hate myself.
I could be me at thirteen or eighteen,
but I am fat, six,
deeply aware that we are given the world and each other
and no wonder we're lonely.

                    But what is TV if not a screen
where light divides down,
where particles charge and involve us
and we are kissed awake
from one native sorrow to another's
just because we are watching? We're alive.

                    And Oswald,
that fox-faced, want-faced man
makes a sudden deep
O with his mouth in our living room because
he has not fallen down yet.
It is the astonishing first kiss
of a bullet in the gut.
That look of mortal surprise

married to a singular understanding, too late,
that (*a*) he was never alone enough, but now
might be forever; (*b*)
was never given enough attention, but now
might be forever—no matter how hard he tries—
or (*c*) all of the above,

                    and like Wile E. Coyote
                                walking on air
a thousand feet above the loco canyon,
Oswald has only to look at the camera, look down,
and he will accomplish
what falls to us all to do, sooner or later.
Commit himself to circumstance
in a thin *yelp!* and puff of smoke.
He is not alone.
There is Ruby with his cocked fedora and
thrust gift, the Dallas cops
who sway slightly, yearning backwards because
there is no way to keep chaos
from becoming panic, and panic in turn
becoming our personal history
of loss and bitter resignation.

                        The hard and hungry world
slips gears, revs: Oswald dies, live remote.
In the wash of breath coming back
the blackened eye of CBS appears.
Station identification
a woman wearing so much mascara
she'd rather do anything but blink.
Even I look up from my book
which by now is a daydream

about Sue Barton, *nurse extraordinaire,* who heals
with clean hands
and without pettiness,
who dates the handsome doctors, and my mother
groaning and bending now from her big
impossible belly.
She holds a dishrag to her eyes, dishrag of belief, and I
receive the family signal,
run to each of my brothers and kiss them
hard on the lips to make them scream.

CINDERELLA AND LAZARUS, PART II

And all the question marks began singing of God's being.
—Tomas Tranströmer, "C Major"

"If the crown fits, wear it," the Prince always crowed.

Have a heart, the moon says now, the same one
the dish & the cow & the spoon
had dealings with.

One life's enough for anyone.

Did we mention that we began in ashes?
Bone-grave, small town,

our mourning mothers and sisters swatted back
the way a white horse
swats heat, sometimes hitting a fly;

later our gramophone, prized possession,
stiffened to a morning glory
with rigor mortis.
The wind roared like nothing in our ears, then nothing.
Kidney pills for kidney stones.

Forty years we've gone on dancing.
The shoe's on the other foot,
but we are always exactly the same couple

in original rags
older than God, than dirt,

doing the Lindy, the Bop, the oh
restless for consummation tango.
Not now death; but now, *now*.

Even his hands spoke in radical tongues.

AT THE PIONEER VALLEY LEGAL CLINIC

All eyes are lowered
in the waiting room of my final visit.
Xerox machines whir,
operating like any human heart
by lights and memory
next time, next time, next . . .
From down the hall
a lecture sponsored by the Whiplash Club,
"Why Pain Does Not Make Us Special."

The clock ticks out Emergency
in minutes. All morning
I have carried what is left of my marriage
in a strongbox rusted, come
slightly unhinged.
It isn't heavy. Inside,
disappointment weighs nothing more
than, say, a child's pink bunny jacket
with its own two sleeves
tied together.

Now in the narrow
plastic seat hooked to all the others
as if this were an airport
or parochial school, I'm shifting, anxious
for what lies waiting
on the other side of a dotted line.
When a lawyer with hair blue as gunmetal bends close,
eyes full of rented grief,
I know what to do.

I say No Fault.
For once I do not call it train wreck, cruel
cosmic prank or house on fire.
I say, "I believe in precision
beyond blame, and second chances—
even those unasked for—
can be legal, binding."
I say, "Party of the first part."
I say, "We are all adults here," and when I do
parolees nodding off in the corner
moan a little, stirring,
the white perfume of documents
rising fiercely from their wrists.

NINE OF CLUBS, CLEVELAND, OHIO
Thursday night: Progressive
Friday and Saturday nights: Eurostyle

Now I know there are bored, beautiful people everywhere.
The boys on their long stems of bones
waft and mingle, sipping Campari,

saying next to nothing to the girls.
Ecstasy is draining.
So is awe, anger, dread, tenderness

when frustrated by convention—any number of emotions
we will not see here tonight,
though we stand equidistant from dancefloor

and Lake Erie, gone back to solution this March
the way a bruise leaves a body.
All night ice loosens and grinds toward Canada.

We feel it more than hear,
and ore boats steer darkly
into the issuance of their lights, their names, as we did

not one hour ago, supplicants in the doorway's
jittery neon. We paid eight dollars to enter
what is spare, cool, clean.

We left behind fish stink and diesel fuel.
But what Europe is this?
Like the music, the dancers' faces

would give no clues. They are whiter than pain
or distraction; their arms dovetail as though
beneath black turtlenecks

a cavity waited, red and humming, for larval wings
to fold twice, re-enter.
I think this is the end of immigration.

I think if a live pig were thrown
skating and shitting onto the gorgeous dancefloor,
no one would stop posing, or crouch down,

knife between his teeth
and stroking the smooth parquet croon
hunger, hunger, hunger

in his blood's first language.
The suburbs have given back their angels.
Refineries rise then sink like wedding cakes

into the filthy river—we've seen it often enough—
and it is wrongheaded or lachrymose
to wish the Old World back as well,

with its babushkas and lamentations, prayer cloths,
boats reeking of garlic cloves
by which we washed up on these shores. And the scythe

whistling at its uppermost arc—
"Di Provenza il mar, il suol."
The shining field,

the ugly babies in the architecture
puffing their thousand-year cheeks at us: I think
it wasn't ours, the past, and now

will never be, who left for better footing,
this purchase on brighter, quicker ground.
No tourist is ever innocent.

Tonight the music churns from hip to hip. The strobe light
won't make up its mind, but flickering hi-speed
erases half of all we see.

It's almost fun, this dancing.
And after, if the foreheads of the warehouses loom down
like character actors whose names

we're forever forgetting, say Ma Joad
or the Little Rascal's truant officer, that's okay.
We're lucky. Our car is right where we left it.

We're tired, sure. A little drunk.
The windshield weeps in a circle of streetlamp light and fog,
but we can drive all night if we want,

lose the lake lolling between these buildings
like a coated tongue,
head south to Akron or Columbus, or Xenia,

anywhere people routinely rise
from the absence of themselves, and begin the day new.
As we will here tonight in the tiny

bathroom crowded with our tribe and generation
bowing to mirrors,
the glimpse of smokey, downturned faces—
you, me, in ritual greeting to our neatly razored lines.

COMEUPPANCE
for Michael, fallen through a skylight

Your enemies call it comeuppance
and relish the details
of a drug too fine, how long
you must have dangled there beside yourself.
In the middle distance of your
twenty-ninth year, night split open
like a fighter's bruised palm,
a purple ripeness.

Friends shook their heads.
With you it was always
the next attractive trouble,
as if an arranged marriage had been made
in a country of wing walkers, lion tamers,
choirboys leaping from bellpulls
into the high numb glitter, and you,
born with the breath of wild on your tongue
brash as gin.

True, it was charming for a while.
Your devil's balance, your debts.
Then no one was laughing.
Hypodermic needles and cash registers
emptied themselves in your presence.
Cars went head-on.
Sympathy, old motor, ran out
or we grew old, our tongues
wearing little grooves in our mouths
clucking disappointment.

Michael, what pulled you up
by upstart roots
and set you packing,
left the rest of us here, body-heavy
on the edge of our pews.
Over the Reverend's lament
we could still hear laughter, your mustache
the angled black wings
of a perfect crow. Later
we taught ourselves the proper method for mourning
haphazard life: salt, tequila, lemon.
Drinking and drifting
in your honor we barely felt a thing.

CHIN MUSIC

I

Watch. My father is about to get knocked on his ass
crossing the playing fields behind Fredonia High School,
Fredonia, New York, where for once
Lake Erie holds to the wrecked shore,
the sky drifts blue and he isn't
punching a fist into his catcher's mitt,
that big dumb ear.
It is April 1945; practice over.
His cleats give him the dancing, half-tough
gait of a boy earth loves
a full second more than the rest of us, and why not?
Outfield's given up its ice
for mud, new-minted green, and my father
is lovely and angry and believes
he will live this way forever,
pinned to the longing for Bunny
Ritowsky under his hands, in his mouth,
while the vineyards murmur and cleave to their wire
and the steel mill confers its one
shadow through the backseat, through them.

II

What we don't know will hurt us,
but not yet. Tomorrow
is a tease, forever gaining in accuracy
what it lacks in momentum,

rising and falling, setting us up like dust
in the bright crosshairs.
Worse, when the future comes we hardly ever hear it.
Like the perfect green recruit
marched straight from central casting into mortar fire
before the first reel is over.
Someone named Petey or JoJo
yells *Duck!* What's the difference?
The ground comes up, the black stars of blood
pop in our mouths like flashbulbs.
We land with our arms shrugged as if
we were fresh out of money or information.

III

Actually, a discus hits my father. Ordinary lead.
The force should kill him but he wakes
in the janitor's room,
a dozen hands throbbing ice water
in stinging slaps against his cheek.
He swims toward the hammered surface, sputters—
already pain is making him famous!
Horse-smell of liniment, sweat, and the huge
furnace breathing;
something in the boy rises to meet
that hot voice of care:
*forget this town, this small-hearted life
you were meant to leave.* And it's all true
if he can just raise himself to his elbows
or stop vomiting.

Then everything hushes, no one
looking at him at all, the tide of the room
pulled by the half moon of the radio's speaker
sobbing, *Ladies, Gentlemen, the President,*
Our beloved President. Then the bells ring for real.
The country begins its long
reeling into death and my father's life begins.

VACATION, 1969

Brothers rolling around in the big back seat,
all elbows and skirmishes,
complaints roared across Mt. Rushmore,
that hard family portrait,
across the Badlands purple with heat.
Back home, black children looted fire hydrants
under sinus-gray skies.
Our trailer was a cracker box ready to jackknife
when my sister, good reader,
practiced her phonetics: nā'päm.

I think it was just outside Turlock, California,
that I grew too sullen
for togetherness.
Rocking my new breasts in my arms,
I was conked out by hormones and Mick Jagger,
my face held in acne's blue siege.
So I pulled up oars early that August,
slept while the boys knocked heads
and my iron-eyed parents took turns
lashed to the wheel,
America, by God, filling the car windows.

LIFTING

If muscles are the currency of dreams,
you are flesh life
curator of the New World, bowing
to nothing but these iron notes.
Sweat, heft, shoulder, thigh, lunge.
Because you wear yourself like a suit
I could never afford, my arms
strain and pretend.
My breath falls through its own trapdoor.

I who have said, *let the thing be what it is.*
Who fed popular children
coins of attention, held down
the cowed corners of my eighth-grade dances.
Who was born like all homely girls
old enough to know better—
I asked you once
what was it like to grow up handsome,
meaning loved. Just now

I've forgotten your answer.
In this garage, where wrecked cans of motor oil
compete with garden tools
for a dying season,
you row the silver barbell up
and I'm meant to see everything injures.
The speed bag is a teardrop
coming back too fast, the heavy bag
a punch-drunk promise,
Everlast in bright red letters.

If a man bench-pressing twice his weight
could lift himself and one other
up, safe above all harm—
but he cannot. One night
on the right-hand side of smoke,
our bodies set out for their true country.
Our bones will collapse, one into the other,
mine into yours as
cheap traveling cups do.

Take a sip. That was my mother
pressing a glass of water into my hands
and the words as she knelt by my bed
were told to comfort.
Her story was simple and thus lost on me,
all about an ugly duckling and a guardian angel
with a funny sense of timing.

I remember her tone, *forbear,*
her face haggard with love as she said it.
But what if the articulate stands
in front of us now, golden and flexing,
bored as any god?
All our years in a hard won mirror!
Reverse transcendence,
I keep lifting,
vow I am almost ready to put foolish things down.

RENOIR'S THE LUNCHEON
OF THE BOATING PARTY

They stay, the mademoiselle
saying O O O to her petit chien,
and the dull-witted boatman who is always
about to speak—who still believes
he will get that chance—
and the ones he has brought here
to La Mère Fourmaise
in washed silks and petit point lace,
chins tilted up and eyelids
dropped with the perfect velocity of flirtation
for over one hundred years.

They stay. And each moment smiling
is like the last five before the bell-ring
in that old grade school,
Notre Dame des Mathématiques Perpétuelles.

There is no other way to explain it.
Pleasure has become their authentic fate.
Not even that expensive charm bracelet, the Seine,
or the soft ripe cheese
or grapes so cold and full of October
can console them.

They want meat with the blood still running.
To feel drunker than they do
right now, to act disgraceful.

They want to oar thin arms into the white
margin of the museum catalog;
once set adrift like Chagall's
elongated angels, they want to haunt
other paintings, become
a shock of Van Gogh wheat
or the cockeyed red freckle on a Picasso tit.

Look. The woman they call "lovely spider"
is stopping her ears with her
black-gloved fingers.
She'd tell you if she could
what it is like to hear over the violin's
held note of civility,
mastheads ringing on all those sailboats
no bigger than sharks' teeth:
one tolling each time someone says,
"I have what I wanted,
and it is not enough."

THE JUDAS CLOCK

After seeing God's mother
on a sidewalk in Buffalo one April,
my great-grandfather had it made:
cloisonné, inlaid ivory stars,
the gilded phases of the moon.
On the hour the upholsterers in his shop
would gather, dumbfounded,
as twelve handpainted apostles
circled the blue throat of that clock.
Each stopped once to bow
his small mechanical head; all but Judas,
who carried rope and silver
back into the humming works.
And all but Grandpa Bert, who would not stop
his curses or his hammering to watch.

This month the rain turns its black wheel
against my bedroom window.
My teeth wake at odd hours, throbbing.
Earthworms knot and slick the garden
and last night I dreamed
you back, Bert Maggio,
wearing death's leather apron and tools.
Standing at the foot of my bed, you saw me
through the wrong end of a telescope,
all that was likely and unlikely
in your immigrant life, come true.
Perturbed, you asked for something
I could not deliver.
A glass of red ocean, I think you said.

One year taught you English enough.
But it was fifty years not knowing
how to dress for spring in western New York,
where steamheat bled the walls
and a pair of long johns
gossiped against the radiator into May.
Your young wife crying—
"When, when home?" In my dream
the language you spoke
was again beautiful, wrong for this life.

Hard luck and responsibility,
I won't bother you again, or try explaining
these midnights spent in a dark kitchen,
only the stove's clock radiant.
It took so little to make you happy.
Cambric, horsehair, three-penny nails
and once a year, a stand of flowering dogwood
you walked into and out of
on your way to Niagara Avenue,
head down now, because one miracle you said
was enough for a working man.
Grandfather, I still want to be like you
but not tonight. Tonight
I'm listening to the rain as it hangs
in the pawnshop of those brief trees
asking for everything,
and in my garden larvae like needles
curved and black, small and stitching
into the green life you freely gave.

MYSTERY

Their words harden in the turning air,
little earrings of light.
I saw, I hate, you never.
Ashtrays and pillows begin to orbit the room.
Whatever furniture they have
rears up on hind legs and howls.

Not even the stove's clock
can catch its breath when they argue.
Its arms windmill, making
the seasons slip a cog.
A buckeye tree in the yard goes
green to burnt orange in a matter of minutes.
Their dog turns suddenly old and blind
and cannot read the book of a dead sparrow
held open in its paws.

Later, the couple kiss
like guests on a television talk show,
expecting nothing.
Whatever they fought about is a mystery to them now.
The wife heads for the kitchen,
sets back the clock, while her husband
demagnetizes the steak knives.
Even their dog remembers its old trick
as it romps in the dark yard.
Play dead, then retrieve, retrieve,
the calm rising all around the house
like a blood pressure.

LAST NAMES

for my sister

I

Oldest child, she was adopted
before doctors could reinvent our mother
whose "woman's problem" in 1955
was a kind of suitcase locked
since the honeymoon in the Poconos.
And because having no children then
was a small death,
my mother grieved until
thick vines shot out from that stone
of a uterus, reeling my sister in.

Later, my brothers and I
took the plainer name, "natural born."
We knew Ellen had come
from the fiery eye of the ballerina
pirouetting in a child's jewelry case,
or from the pursed lips of certain
squash blossoms—
any birth without pain was magic.

Bossy fairy-tale sister, she could do
no wrong. In her games
we played minor characters:
a frog, ugly witch, thicket of roses.
In secret, my brothers and I played pranks.

We lined up our jealousy like toy howitzers
at the foot of blue iron beds,
not knowing the years of night
she would have to rock herself in the dark,
mumbling her thousand
possible names.

II

Tonight, in this restaurant,
I want to put down my wine glass, touch
my sister's elbow and say
you have always been one of us.
But my tongue chips away at something
breakable, the air like shale,
thin layers revealing
the ordinary half-truths we've survived on
for so long. So I listen
to stories about the fifth-grade class
she teaches, how a children's book
named *Deanie* mentions masturbation.
How everything we grew up with has changed.

Once I overheard my mother say
better if she had adopted all her children.
She was tired and envied
the slender women she saw on TV.
Since then I have never left
one place for another feeling entirely safe.
Leaving Ellen tonight,
I'll imagine that alternate universe

where I am worse than orphaned,
one of the never born,
almost-daughter of a woman who finds
Jesus instead, or of a coal miner
who never makes it back from the earth
to his life.

All memory of me shrivels to blue gas.
My last name creaks on sour hinges
over the abandoned guesthouse,
Vacancy, No Vacancy.
When a red ball with gold stripes
bounces into the street,
I have not rolled it there: the wind
forgets me easily, moves on.
Foxgrape, bluebearded iris,
the notched green of simple weeds swirls up
where I used to stand.
There is nothing else left, not love,
but only its possibility,
my sister and I
untouched by all that might have been.

VENICE BEACH: BRIEF SONG

Maybe Zizi is right.
Rocket a mile up, look back,

and we're all just earthlings in restaurants
talking low, trying to figure

one thing out, or
stop one thing from happening.

And all the crystal meth in the world
cannot lift even one of our bodies

free of this argument, or set us clear
of the boardwalk's great

stake in pleasure. Still
the hypodermic shadow of the Capitol Records Building

is oddly comforting,
and the Sufi on rollerskates

promises the next tune is ours
on a boom box he's hoisted

like huge hope to his many-robed shoulder:
Bix Beiderbecke and the boys,

"I'm Coming Virginia."
This is not the life we requisitioned for.

But what can we do now that we're here?
When Larry leaves, when Frances

makes her final point and leaves,
and Zizi never showed (she had something to frame),

I know what I'll do.
Contrive a window like this one

where I'll lean out in the old, theatrical
self-wounding way—oh the buoy bells

of loneliness! Oh the black
candles under waves!—but still

tasting cooler air on my face
like a fire hydrant blowing.

Like a different promise.
Then I'll bless the heads of the insane skateboarders,

those little dooms in their
acid-orange knee pads.

Last night they kept me awake
with their breakneck wheels, their passion. Tonight

I'll watch them marry the pit
city fathers laid years ago, and imagining that

gesture of local
wisdom or submission

will be like imagining this prayer for a change:
to be truly blonde, and just once

blown away, flying and flying and flying.

FOR DOMENIC, MY 1970S

A decade so ugly
it doesn't matter what you wear,
you wear it daily for weeks: watch cap and sideburns,
a pair of low-slung
biker boots and jeans.
Going as far as you can go and still come back
seems a worthwhile motto.
You say it now,
scrubbing your hair from your eyes
with a monkey wrench.
But the war's over.
The President decamped
to one of dignity's lesser branch offices.
Even the Perfume River you imagine
flowing backwards to a source that makes

more sense than any of the roads you've chosen.
Everyone has their ghosts.
Out here, lost between Chula Vista
and the shit-for-luck
hood of this Ford, alone, inconsolable
(no smokes since noon!),
yours is the sun so hot it's a noise
everywhere inside you.
Like toothache or heartache:
a plow strikes a stone
somewhere near Bloomington,
and you launch that Budweiser at the dining room wall
all over again, to make a point.

Your father yelling something about Communists
and coronaries.

Never mind.
Arroyo melts into barrio,
Badlands into high plains as if any gap
or sudden promontory could be filled
by faith and motion alone.
In this way, not going *where,* just going,
you met Sheila—or was it by then
Rainbow Dulcimer Sheila?—
and in a sleeping bag you shared with peyote
big and welcome as the stars,
she proposed a future that seemed, well,
useless to deny.
A freezer, actually.
Model 1076, no-frost, Harvest Gold,
to fit in the back of your station wagon,
where, without benefit of license,
you'd sell fudgesicles and creamsicles
together forever.
Live on tamales and Tecate and fine stone love.
Throw the empties in the back, amen.

But Sears keeps *finding* you,
and the sunburn between your fingers
feels like wrath.
On the car radio someone's inducting
misery into the Hall of Fame.
You sing along in Spanish
a love song so wild, so trellised by grief,
it could raise the dead

in their shimmering traces
then fling them, like to like,
in brilliant patterns against the sun.
But not this Ford.
Not this universal joint the old man would eyeball
and in his slow, Republican,
unending way,
know how to fix.

The trouble with you, Domenic,
Rainbow Sheila said
that last night in San Bernardino,
is you keep getting The Good Thief mixed-up
with The Thief in the Night.
When you asked her,
running your hand through your hair and trying
not to think it, *thinner today,*
just what the hell that meant,
she shook her head.
"Asking forgiveness, man, is dead."
She shook then folded her tiger panties
in triangles for the long ride.
Outside, someone named Garth
revving and sputtering
a luckless Harley rage.
Ten years from writing or waking
beloved in the world, you'd never felt so tired
or alive to one good idea,
though what it was,
you couldn't exactly say.

That's alright. Soon enough
you'll have to trash this dream,
throw the monkey wrench
like a shaman's medicine-bone on the blink
end over end into cholla and weeds,
start walking.
The ice cream's melting.
Sit down, Domenic. What we do to stay alive
is different from what we are,
and some things are lost
so well we won't ever have to lose them again.
Here in the long end of the smug, bankable eighties,
I want to remember you this way,
chin in your hands, a little
teary-eyed watching
thin rivulets form down the bumper in the dust.
Watching for the fire ants
that come, like you,
to carry what sweetness they can on their backs
toward nothing we can see
here in the distance, just across the border.

December 1988

BOMBAY HOOK WILDLIFE REFUGE

Past the dull, slack-jawéd barns
of lower Delaware, cornfields
have knelt down for the year, and cows
glazed with cold do nothing
as we pass in your husband's late model Buick.
I am the relative relatives sent
to comfort. Still mourning,
you grow nervous with my small talk—
woolens, a Black Watch scarf you sent me once—
though I notice too late
your own clothes have given up on you.

Crabshacks and winter yachts
hang their lights over Delaware Bay;
scrub pines lean into wind—
fine, dangerous points.
In this car where we seem to float,
not talking, cut off, as if we had left the ground
lighter by two people,
I do not have to remind myself
how they found you once, the river
flared over your head like a black skirt.
Always you spoke with those intelligent
hawk's eyes, warning me off:
so much not to learn.

The moon is up, a slipped skin.
There is a sign half hidden by marsh grass
that pokes its fingers through the moon,
Dismantle, Case All Guns.

For a moment your hand whitens my wrist
and I wonder, not why we are here,
but how many shoulders you've held or shaken until
love heated your forehead, anger
divided its cells beneath your breasts.

For an hour we ride like this
without guarantees. And if deer
or blue heron or the geese that pull
seasons in behind them are here,
we don't spot any, or anything else
to tell us this is safety.
There is just the afternoon gone threadbare,
the bite of sand under tires,
something swirled in a coffee cup.

THE REGISTRY OF WALLS AND EDGES

In the hour of luminous change
between a little roast beef
and a little TV, cop shows pouring

gray light across the walls, us,
more than once in that hour
have we dawdled on the front stoop to worry

about love. Where it all ends.
That tidal emotion.
Sweet getting close, followed

by sweeter getting away.
Love fades, we say, shrugging as though
we'd hit on the real reason

the undead walk among us
only to lose their sad, bewildered
faces in a mirror. Or why our mothers

carried aspirin for years
in the bottoms of purses,
though what's solid surely wears away

to nothing in no time: white dust, a speck of lint
where the raised letters used to be.
But isn't making love itself

most blurring?
Swap meet of hands and tongues,
the mutual fretwork, the long

living in each other's mouths, after which
we fall back to separate lines
in our double beds and breathe, and no wonder

our clear breath becomes
a registry of walls and edges.
Maybe the woman cries—

neither happy nor unhappy.
The man smokes and counts
pom-poms on homemade curtains, or else he

pats the woman's smooth flank to say
"there, there,"
as if the loneliness we'll soon be courting

could be airlifted somewhere else,
the upper right-hand sock drawer, perhaps.
Still, it works. Kissing once,

we turn our pillows to a cooler side and sleep.
We like it this way,
missing each other now

with an easy camaraderie
found sometimes between war buddies or strangers
who've seen the same freak accident,

and after, walk up the beach together,
tacking into wind.
"Has everything been done that could be done?"

We'll ask it over and over.
But our hands are birds called home
in hard weather, in this moment

before parting when we gesture back
flutteringly, toward the small
lone figure

receding in the ocean's swells: out of earshot,
asleep on his raft,
happy for all we know.

RED-EYE FLIGHT

Love. The Family. Grief grows black
then green on that horizon
as day begins all over again, on a far
adult coast, where light is expanding
like the pages of this book

someone's dropped into rose-scented bathwater.
The Book of Hapless Motherhood.
And the children at the bolted door,
should they pound or fly for help?
They love her so much!

This poem scares me. It goes and comes back.
It whirs under the too-tight memory
someone else started, but I make portable as worry
and carry here tonight.
Below me the Rockies must be melted-down

black candle wax—I've flown over them enough—
and in other places mounded up
where a woman could stand in theory and reckon
back to a mother and a danger she understood.
Mother of needs. Mother of every self-

protecting self-love;
if she shrugged us off like weak water from her long
black hair, she had shopping or napping,
it was the female thing to do.
If my sister and I bashed each other

with driftwood, broomsticks,
whatever was handy or at least brutal
beyond reference,
we did it until we beat the words right out of each other,
love, the family, grief that never gets taken back.

Then she passed us over.
A cool shadow in the shape of a plane,
wings tipped: brief salute.
A woman with her arms opened so empty and wide
you'd swear it was the transept and nave

of the Church of No Asking. For Anything. Goosebumps—
we fell into line.
Tonight it's morning where I'm going.
But up here, out my dim particular porthole,
it's dark as the words these businessmen

keep sighing in their sleep.
To the sound of our bunched-up breathing,
to the engine's high reeds, my heart has swiveled
closer to one darkness
inside my skin. But I'm not there yet.

I'm scared from drinking too many miniature wines
and I'm crying, though softly
so the closest strangers
won't hear. I love my life it seems
and don't want to die this way

counting the wing's one obsessively pulsating
pulmonary light, and then
my little brothers the stars
with everything figured out—still way ahead of me.
Their hunger makes holes in the master plan.

They're sticking out their brilliant-pink fiery tongues
and singing *me me me* to that reticence
the fading night, and to all the days coming on
without permission, like us,
raw and raging and beautiful as greed.

THE HOLE IN THE CEILING

Bent at the waist
at the head of the class,
St. Sebastian rolls his eyes.
Like Jesus, he is not dead yet.
He grips the arrow in his chest as though he were
afraid of losing it.
Like your best baby doll
he might moan outright, when tilted,
from somewhere deep in the belly.

Love wills this cursive and this long division!
In the science corner
pole beans uncork their wobbly heads
under wet paper towels.
A spider walks on its eight legs forward—
tiny unlit chandelier.
By recess you are swabbed by God,
soaked through in your deadly uniforms.

Children, today's lesson is goodness.
Or did we leave off at suffering,
goodness's twin?
The nun with the kewpie pout and high starched forehead
has some answers. Behold
the stain on the ceiling.
Plaster wavelets of gray meringue: by June
we will chart mold's progress
like the shape of restlessness, like sin
behind it, some dark
repetition of water.

HONEYMOON OCEAN, 1939

There is a way the mind shimmers up
and your mother finds it by counting
naked ladies on a lampshade.
They're passing gold balls between them endlessly,
wavey as mermaids with knees
crooked in some attitude of pleasure
found only on the boardwalk, Wildwood, New Jersey.

Outside, regular stars are plinking
a music cold as bedsprings.
The Atlantic, honeymoon ocean, bends forward
to brush its hair.
Salt drifts along the floor in patterns
gritty as lace;
it will never be over, then is

and he rolls off, big dumb galoot.
He likes the next part, too: twitching into sleep
the way a man might reading
Prince Valiant to himself,
moving his lips.
He wipes his cock on the flowered sheet and grins.

Even the bed retracts in this tourist cabin.
It's a way to heal the wall each morning.
But what of the other one,
little souvenir?

Where love makes no plan
past the first, no provision for candles
or sandbags or the hundred
natural disasters of the heart,
love also rises, an island on fire.

There's a light in the cramped bathroom
and your mother finds it,
globe green and brain-shaped.
Later she'll say she didn't know
anything that night. Not how far or where.
Just that the moon snores belly up,
she needs a cigarette, a drink,

and trembling, knocks a spider loose from its damp
precarious sway. She hits it
smack! with the palm of her hand. Then
because she is young, not desperate,
watches without blinking
as a thousand spiders escape in waves
tiny as light if light
were your first words spinning away from her
across black diamond tile.

CALVIN COOLIDGE ASLEEP

Even now he has nothing to say.
No snoring, no muttered confession of flappers
named Pearl or Daisy.
Aides tiptoe around the greatdesk
where his head bobs on crossed arms,
a bubble of saliva
ticking on presidential lips.
In the corner, his mechanical horse waits,
silent on its springs.

Let the world wait, too. Eugene Debs,
Sacco and Vanzetti, knives that splash
in bloodfields of Nicaragua
and Mexico: like a fountain turned suddenly off,
the President has receded into himself
then rises. This time
not in the Vermont of his childhood
where he hid alone for hours
beneath tall hollyhock, and where everyone
is equally dull and understands
hasty words ignite like barns
full of green hay. Not,
thank heaven, in bluestockinged Amherst,
where frat boys in raccoon coats
speak their secret dialect of ease.

No. This time
it is a saloon in Abilene, Texas,
in the unlikely country of his imagination
before last century turned.

He pounds the bar
and a table of gamblers slink out.
A shot of amber bourbon, rare flower,
blooms in his fist.
Outside, there are no constituents or speeches,
just a thousand head of cattle
waiting, dumb behind their blunt
brown faces.

What wakes him finally
he can't say. Sheer happiness,
or the runaway carriage of prosperity ringing
down Pennsylvania Avenue.
Or maybe it is the Great Depression, hunched
and breathing at the edge of his life—
its yellow eyes.
More likely it is one of his aides
signaling time to plant a tree
in the Rose Garden with Grace.
The reporters are waiting.
Coolidge scowls. Runs a hand through thin hair,
"There are Reds in our women's colleges."

LARGE FAMILIES

Late August,
no breeze rifling its feathers,
and still the robin turned and turned in sunlight.
By the time we found it, head lolled,
hung from a low branch,
its eyes were fastened shut with lice.
The red bandanna of a throat was empty.
I was eleven then but knew
freak accidents when I saw them.
Higher in the black walnut tree was a nest
half built, stitched with kite tails
and abandoned string,
                  and when my brothers
in ruined brown schoolshoes
tried to whack at the bird with their sticks
as though it were a Christmas *piñata,*
my father, a tired man, stopped them.
He hauled out a wooden ladder, climbed that calamity,
then sat for a long time in the branches
holding the dead bird in his hands.
And the robin all the while
holding her breath of blue eggs.

THREE OR FOUR STARS,
THE FAR-BRANCHING BARK OF A DOG

The social workers have named it
a family matter, this love
that leaves marks.
Without expertise, I set it down,
how neighbors reported smoke
and the sound of a typewriter
which was really the little girl's heels
drumming when she felt first heat.
How the teenage mother
and that boyfriend—some would-be drifter, some
hilljack machinist laid off
not three days before—
cranked up the gospel tunes
then held their shoulders against the oven door
until dishes stopped ringing
in the cupboards:
devil's glamour lived
behind a four-year-old's eyes.
How the firemen who answered the call
now report odd moments of weeping,
the inability to maintain an erection,
which is also a family matter.
And that the day I heard this story on the news
I was all night trying to sleep
with the lights on
because, small good that it does them,
the brutally dead
possess our remembering.

Under leftover stars and the far-branching
bark of a dog,
I went out into the backyard
to sweat out dawn.
It was October in New England and I needed
to remember how to breathe,
my own childhood safe
five states away, pressed after years
by the weight of who knows
what blessing into
not diamonds, but a pill
to take with scotch in that veering hour
against my doctor's wishes.

LATE SUMMER NEWS

Applications are now being accepted for public burning.
— radio announcement, Charlotte, N.C.

Come over here from over there, girl.
— Bob Dylan, "Don't Fall Apart on Me Tonight"

Up and down this red clay route
where heat makes waves, mailboxes
hold a stiff salute above the chokeweed:
today, against all odds,
someone has remembered you.
My hand tests the little oven.
Visa, J. C. Penney, Southern Bell, these mornings I confess
I'm happy to find bills there
or anything bearing my name
plain as light through a wax paper window.
"Pledge to the Radical Gay Alliance,"
"Plant a Tree in Israel,"
even the stacked deck of other people's needs
I read lovingly. Then this:
an envelope, flatbread and salt,
from a friend who writes for nothing I can give.
J & L Steel turns the air orange, she says,
in the old neighborhood.
Bag ladies shamble up and down Murray Avenue,
still speaking to the personal angels
who live in their coat pockets,
and caged live chickens
bask in Neederman's doorway, waiting to be delivered
unto the butcher and the rabbi.

"What I mean most is that laughter
won't be the same without you."
Her daughter, she closes, has grown gorgeous
and last month married for love.

Who knows what to wish for?
The big picture hides in its own wide margins—
no one sees it or why
we sign our names to each day that comes
wearing its New Wave fashions.
But when the white parachute of faith or memory blooms
backward from this letter in my hand,
I'm ready for it, am meant to see
projected in its pure, billowing center
how the blind really do lead us.
There, my father in his catcher's squat in 1946,
a Tareyton dangling from his lips—
his slow, loopy charm.
My mother at Sacred Heart High
taking lessons in resisting charm, fingers crossed.
My Italian grandfather kneeling
to his 80th garden, basil, fennel, chard;
my Irish grandfather's cancer
thriving like a wrung note in his vocal chords.
Friends, I see them, too,
playing air guitars and clinking bottles of Iron City
against Mouton Rothschild, 1976.
If choices were wood
I could build a bridge back to them
with the choices I've made to be here.
I could burn one down.
This morning, head tilted, I think

I must look for all the world
like that RCA dog, full of dopey trust and waiting.
The gravel makes a noise under my feet
like just-thrown dice, and
what silk there is floats away from me
over hundred-year pines,
all the bright strings attached.

MINIATURE GOLF
for Chuck

It looks easy enough.
The grip and the nature of the lie.
Hazard where a church—by accident or old, opposing
    designs—
is a wishing well one stroke,
a guillotine the next.
And the giant chipmunk's tail
sweeping and sweeping
the stupid ball further from the hole.

Which is to say
miniature golf is *not* desire, but so close
you can hear it in the omen
Coke machine's rumble,
the mosquitoes' plaintive airs & violins.
Joy is such a simple obsession
we'll never get it right.
But what we wouldn't give

to be this big all the time.
Forgive the world
we drive away from August nights
to the frail cries of children swinging clubs,
our bright relentless chipping
after pleasure.
Heading home then, beat, tired, score settled,

how like the annunciating angel
that chipmunk would seem
in our rearview mirrors.
As if life had grown undeniably fair
in relation to our worst shot,
and how far we still had to go,

and tender, exacting,
it raised a radiant paw to bless us forward.
Be not afraid.
You're on your own now, yes, but trust me!
Even the tricky part's
a piece of cake.

FORMICA

Little flute, who will play you now?
The penis bone of a whale looks
lonely you think, perplexed, frugal, and you say so
though even small sounds
bring guards in carpet slippers running.

The world will never love us enough.
On a Sunday when it rains and we visit
museums, this seems true.
In the west wing's Whaling Village Exhibit & Diorama,
the killer shark is tiny.
We could pop him in our mouths. Suck and suck
until forgiveness were nothing

but a fierce candy going sweet
then sour on the tongue.
The side eye rolling white, intimate, indifferent
with indifferent blood,
but it is only at the center that we see
a concentrate of our sadness
like a lifetime supply of vitamin pills

melting down.
Love, last night I held your heated skull
as I would a projector between my hands,
tenderly, and gingerly.
You weren't a fancy machine then,
but a Super-8 pouring home
movies of cars' thin shadows against our bedroom wall;

the faster they ran
the antique dresser to the end of our turning block,
the more fascination leaving had for me.
As though history, while we sleep or dream
another's sleeping for him,
could be held off—detoured—
from even one second's worth of gearing

and swift abiding inside our skins.
As if the important dates
weren't memorizing *us*.
The hieroglyphics are on the wall.
I love you, but we go down into the dirt from here,
uncataloged, scattered,
a thousand grinning ashtray skulls,

not to some Thai restaurant
as formerly imagined, *Gang kiaw wan,*
a spicy treat for those who enjoy
our green curry, although
that's not a bad idea, either, you say.
You are hungry.
You are always so hungry when we are together.

So we head out into the rain
to find a room where tassels
sprout from the jaws of wise, generic dragons.
It is almost March.
The road shines wet and specific
in the taillights of a taxi screeching past, too close,
dragging behind it

red shoelaces of light
and there is nothing to say about any of this.
Not the sudden thaw or the way
our cheap tennis shoes have taken it all in,
flowering outward.
Or that any moment our smiles might connect us
in the old matrimonial way,

wan, vigilant, transubstantial,
they'll say, what are these moments for a species & kind
when Formica is enough?
Easily we will take our place
at the table where skin goes weird
in the buzzing, fluorescing light. And easily
our hands find each other

X-rayed down to smallbones that fit.
The insanely kind waiter
bringing clear fish soup—fish, yes; no heads please—
then glass noodles, coconut beef,
all the while wearing a bow tie beautiful
and so patently absurd
we will only keep nodding back at him,

yes, yes!
Take the shiny menus away.
Ordering anything, we're authorities in the dark.
And all we have to do,
darling, is step off this curb.

THANKSGIVING

The first tilting I owe to a wild cousin
grown bored with dry-run kisses.
Angles the soap operas taught
kept our chins trembling free, but our lips
turned blurry and uneventful
under the haunted plumbing, the rope garlic
hung like sleigh bells in my grandparents' cellar.
"Tongues," she announced finally, brilliant child.
I lay back. No noise.
Dirty floorboards at our elbows, cold, and there
a basket of ashes that yesterday caught
the turkey's red life, one drop at a time.
Cobwebs waved to us in dim motion.
My sweater she lifted up, dust in the rich weave.

Basket of ashes, black bed we lie down in
and lie down in—that afternoon
I knew there was no loneliness
I could not outgrow.
My cousin showed white teeth, yelping joy.
My hands tightened on her shoulders until I felt
Lake Erie, ice-shocked at the breakwall,
begin inching against the lines
of a few crazy fishermen.
Upstairs with animal patience, Aunt Susan
dried dishes. She nodded us toward more apples, more pie.
But *Quietly, Quietly.*
All the uncles' mouths had fallen open.

In front of the television set
they worked off the drug of their heavy meal
while the wide receiver went
long, arms yearning. Nothing could stop him.
He was beamed on the light I called aftermath
years later, into that room where we tiptoed,
girls holding our balance for the sleeping men.

HOW IT COMES

Like the small sound
from across chain link, your briarhopper
neighbor taking a long pull on a Bud,

then spritzing a little on his hibachi
that smokes like an old box camera,
and spraying, too, his pale wife

wearing her zebra-print halter
over breasts full of sway and collapse,
who ricochets

back and forth, back and forth,
pink burger meat between her palms
with such rapt devotion

you see for the first time
what he saw all those summers ago
in the parking lot of the 7-11,

and why this afternoon the Grateful Dead
work their sweet pain just right
on a radio propped in a bathroom window, and why

this hound wears a bandanna and keeps falling
in love with himself in a new way
in a pond of dust—

joy's perennial wild card fan,
obedient to the only words that matter:
Catch! Attaboy!

So that when the delicious gift comes
he will be ready, though it comes
without warning,

like trust after a long uneasiness;
as when you were a child
and sleep took you mid-sentence

under the dome light and low
talk of fireworks going silver to blue in another town, faroff;
and your mother with a cool hand

on your father's sunburned neck as he drove.
The way fidelity still begins
in the backseats of the great, generous
muscle cars of the sixties.

GROUP THERAPY LOUNGE.
COLUMBIA, SOUTH CAROLINA

What is the past, what is it all for?
A mental sandwich?
—John Ashbery, "37 Haiku"

In the end it all comes back
and lucid as this, O sad drinker
of a thousand boo-hoo beers,
O pinball ringing
toward oblivion: oblivion
with its wide white arms and short attention span
will never hold you for long.
Now morning is here. It comes
precise, brutal,
a CPA shaking loose his ledger
of sunlight and bad debts, and you
wake on the sidewalk, still
pretty much hammered.

Never has your breath creaked
with so many fossils.
Your bones ache older than the hills
and there are no hills in Columbia, South Carolina,
just birds in the crape myrtle
singing a song of rubber bands
stretched to breaking.
In the gutter, a few pigeons
bobbing for a lost contact lens.

Isn't this the oldest story?
Sunday, the day we care least about the world
and the newspaper is the fattest.
A Plymouth burns down Bull
to Confederate, rocker panels rusted
and swinging wide—
it barely slows to pitch
a bundle of comics & coupons by your head, right there
on the sidewalk where you've slept
and where you wake, still pretty much hammered.

History repeats itself. Big deal.
You have more pressing problems, for instance,
this cockroach driving by
with grand determination.
He's an emissary from the one species
unafraid of the atom or the anvil, and you
can't move or stop watching.
Doesn't it bring tears to your eyes,
the thought that every minute lying here
you're learning something about yourself,

some news on hot winds borne
across the chapped lip of Southern horizon—
the green spores of remorse
taking root. Soon, you think,
even you will rise under your own power,
vertebrae stacking
much like seasoned cordwood
for the day's big fire,
and your brain issuing directives
to the whole body: go forth, be a man, etcetera.

Soon, not yet.
Imagine the God of gills.
Imagine the time it took those gills to burn
through closed, crude flesh.
Then mud, lungs, twelve or twelve hundred spears
jabbed in rough circles at the sun.
Imagine catfish lately
sprouting legs for the pages of *Scientific American*.
Hope is like that. Blind and bleached white,
revising itself every million years
to climb out of the crazy swamp and live.
At the Used Car Lot
day-glo flags are snapping and popping 24 hours,
and you ride that rhythm
in a prone position. They wave
their mutant arms to you,
and you can't help it, down on the mortal sidewalk—
you wave back, astonished as anyone.

"Nine of Clubs, Cleveland, Ohio": Line 44 refers to a line in the aria "Di Provenza il mar" from Verdi's opera *La Traviata*. In the original scene, Alfred's father attempts to console his heartbroken son by recalling their home in "fair Provence." He appeals to Alfred in vain to return.

"Three or Four Stars, The Far-Branching Bark of a Dog": Lines 26, 27, and 28 are adapted from a paragraph in Robert Pinsky's *The Situation of Poetry* in which he writes, "Beyond the limits and somewhat unexpected contours of the speaker's character is the subject of remembering: how the dead possess our remembering, the small good it does them, and how accidental and sadly bewildering the contact is between historical actions and individual character."

For the poem's title I am indebted to Elton Glaser for a line in his poem "Farmlife in Ohio."